S0-AQL-029

WHEN GOD MADE THE TREE

BY VIRGINIA KROLL
ILLUSTRATED BY
ROBERTA COLLIER-MORALES

DAWN PUBLICATIONS

Dedication

For Edna Keefe, terrific teacher, and
Margery Facklam, marvelous mentor.
—VK

To the people who devote themselves to saving the old growth forests and
rainforests of our planet, and especially to Carolyn and Bill for their help.
—RC-M

Author's note: I realize and respect the belief that God does not have gender or that God is female. Because our language does not have a unisex pronoun besides "it", I have chosen to use the traditional "Him" when referring to God.

Copyright © 1999 Virginia Kroll
Illustrations copyright © 1999 Roberta Collier-Morales

A Sharing Nature With Children Book

All rights reserved. No part of this book may be reproduced or transmitted to any form or by any means, electronic or mechanical, including photocopying, recording, or by any information and retrieval system, without written permission from the publisher.

Library of Congress Cataloging-in-Publication Data

Kroll, Virginia L.
     When God made the tree / by Virginia Kroll ; illustrated by Roberta Collier-Morales. – 1st ed.
     p. cm. – (A Sharing nature with children book)
     Summary: Presents thirteen different tree species around the world and describes how they carry out God's plan by supporting people and animals in a harmonious relationship.
     ISBN: 1-883220-97-1 (case)
     ISBN: 1-883220-96-3 (pbk.)
     1. Trees—Juvenile literature. 2. Trees—Utilization—Juvenile literature. [1. Trees—Religious aspects.} I. Collier-Morales, Roberta, ill. II. Title. III. Series.
QK475.8.K76 1999   99-12163 CIP
582.16—dc21

Dawn Publications
P.O. Box 2010
Nevada City, CA 95959
800-545-7475
Email: inquiries@DawnPub.com
Website: www.DawnPub.com

Printed in Hong Kong

10 9 8 7 6 5 4 3 2 1
First Edition

Computer production by Rob Froelick

rees. How could we live without them?

They give us shade on blistering days
and logs to burn on frigid nights.

They provide wood for homes, furniture, fences, boxes,
baskets, puzzles, toys and musical instruments.

Paper and cloth can be made from their bark. Roofs and
rope can be made from their leaves.

They figure into the holiday celebrations of many
cultures and provide nesting sites for some of our favorite
birds and beasts.

They even help clean the air we breathe and put oxygen
into it.

And the foods! Peaches, plums, cherries, apples, walnuts,
coconuts, figs and more.

God knew all this when He made trees.

When God made the mesquite,
He thought of the cattle
Chewing its pods for fodder,

4

And of Fernando,
Who would use its sticks for fences
To keep his cattle corralled.

When God sowed the saguaro,
    He knew the tiny cactus mouse
    Would make her cozy nest inside its trunk,

And that Lusita would eat the sweet red fruit
That grew from its waxy white blossoms.

hen God put dwarf willows in the hilly soil,
He thought of the mighty musk ox
Staying alive through the bitter winter
By nibbling its brittle branches,

8

And of Umik, who would use the sticks for firewood
To keep her family's igloo aglow.

When God planted the pine,
    He thought of the partridge,
    Burrowed into a bed of fallen needles,

10

And of Laila, preparing dinner dishes
From the nuts inside the cones.

hen God cultivated the coco palm,
He considered the coconut crab
That would scale the trunk
And crack apart the hard, hairy shells.

He thought of sleepy Deepa,
Awakened from a frightening dream,
Sipping coconut milk to calm herself.

hen God made the banana tree,
He thought of the flying foxes
That would feed upon its luscious fruit,

And of Mai, who would pluck a green gigantic leaf
To use as an umbrella.

When God made the eucalyptus,
He counted on the koala
To munch its fragrant leaves,

16

And knew that Lauren and Luke would need
Cough drops and cold syrup, made from its oils,
When flu season came around.

 hen God seeded the fig,
    He had monkeys in mind,
    For they would feast on the fleshy fruit.

He thought of baby Bobo as well,
Bundled in a soft bark-cloth blanket
That his father made from the tree trunk's inner layer.

**W**hen God made the baobab,
He blessed the bushbaby
That would lick the sticky pollen
From the sweet, snowy blossoms.

He also blessed Hamidi,
Who helps his family hollow the heavy trunk
For storing rainwater inside.

hen God created yagrumas,
He made a place for the wee coqui frogs
That sing sweet songs from dusk till dawn.

He knew, too, that Francisca and her folks
Would use their lightweight wood
For baskets, crates and boxes.

When God planted the kapok,
He smiled at the pretty parakeets
Splitting open its tasty seeds.

He thought of Ernesto, who would rest his tired head
On a pillow stuffed with the fiber-floss
Of this stately "silk-cotton tree."

W hen God sowed the sweetgum,
He thought of the lime-colored Luna moth,
Whose caterpillars would feed on its foliage,

And of John, Amanda, Melissa, Mark and Katie,
Who would seek a shady spot after playing tag
On a steamy August afternoon.

hen God made the maple,
    He thought of the silver-winged cicadas,
    Strumming their joyful summer song,

And of me,
Climbing high toward the bright blue sky,
Thinking of Him.

The **mesquite** (mesKEET) is a small desert tree or shrub. Its roots grow deep underground in search of water. Its cream-colored flowers yield pale yellow beans containing a sweet-tasting pulp, which farmers feed to their **cattle**. **Fernando** is from Mexico. His father is teaching him how to make corrals for the cattle from mesquite branches. Yesterday Fernando helped two cows give birth to their calves. He felt very grown-up, like a real cattleman.

The giant **saguaro** (saWAro) is a spiny cactus that can grow fifty feet tall and weigh several tons. The pleats in its skin widen after a rain as it soaks in and stores the water. Many creatures scoop out holes for nesting in the saguaro's flesh. One is the **cactus mouse**, a small tan rodent that stores the seeds of the saguaro's fruit. Indian people pull down the red, pulpy fruit with long poles and make jam, candy and syrup from it. **Lusita** belongs to the Tohono O'odham people of the Southwestern U.S. She thinks that the silhouettes of saguaros look like people with their arms extended. Every year, Lusita eagerly looks forward to the saguaro fruit harvest.

Dwarf willows are the only trees that grow in the northernmost areas of tundra, a level Arctic area. They grow in a layer of marsh, which in the summer is on top of permafrost. In the winter, huge hungry **musk oxen** munch the branches which are their only food when the ground is buried in snow. "Igloo" is the Eskimo word for "home," whether that home is a house, an apartment, a trailer, or a temporary tent or ice-block dwelling. **Umik** is an Inuit girl from Alaska. She has brought in a pile of brittle drawf willow sticks to help start the fire in her family's wood-burning stove.

Pines are conifers—cone-bearing trees—whose needle-like leaves stay green year-round. When the needles die, they dry out and fall, forming a think, soft carpet under the tree. Ground-dwelling game birds, such as the **partridge**, often rest on those comfortable carpets. **Laila** is from Lebanon. Tonight she and her family will make kibbi for dinner, the national dish of Lebanon, which is made from lamb, onions, cracked wheat, and—most tasty of all—pine nuts, the seeds from inside the cones.

The **coco palm** produces coconuts. It belongs to a group of tropical and subtropical palm trees that furnish shelter, waxes, oils, food, clothing, fuel and timber. The **coconut crab** is the largest of all land crabs. Also known as the robber crab, it is named for its habit of climbing coco palms to get the nuts. With its strong claws, it cracks their hard shells to eat the white pulp. People eat coconut pulp too, wet and raw or dry and shredded. People also drink coconut milk, the clear fluid that comes from the core of the nut. It is a special tasty treat for **Deepa**, a girl who lives in India.

The **banana tree** is actually a large herb that springs from an underground stem called a rhizome. Flower spikes bloom atop its trunk and turn into bunches of long, flavorful, nourishing treats. There are hundreds of types of banana trees cultivated in hot climates. Leaves of most banana trees are huge. They are used as umbrellas, as their thick surface sheds rain well, or as parasols (sun shades) by people like **Mai**, a girl from the island of Borneo. **Flying foxes** roost in trees by day and fly by night to feed on juicy tropical fruits, such as bananas. Flying foxes are really large bats. With their large eyes and pointed faces, they look like foxes; hence, their name.

Eucalyptus (you-ca-LIP-tuss) trees are native to Australia and New Zealand. Glands in their leaves contain a valuable oil with a distinct aroma, used chiefly in medicines for coughs and colds. Their bark is used in tanning and paper-making. **Koalas** are marsupials (pouched mammals) that, in the wild, feed almost entirely on eucalyptus leaves. **Lauren** and **Luke** are from Australia.

The **fig tree** produces a tasty fruit that is eaten by many animals, including **monkeys**, bats and rodents, as well as humans. In the Ituri rainforest of Central Africa, native peoples make "bark cloth" from the fig tree. They carefully strip away the outer bark to get to the inner layer, then gently take the inner layer too, which they soak and then pound with an elephant tusk until soft. **Bobo** is an Mbuti boy. After Bobo's father made the blanket, his mother and sister decorated it with berry-juice designs, and it was ready for him when he was born.

The **baobab** is often called "tree of life" because of its many uses. Shaped like a huge jug, its bark is essential for making paper, cloth and rope. Its oversized trunk is often hollowed out to hold barrels for collecting rainwater—or to house an entire family! Many creatures like the nectar of its sticky white blossoms. One of these is the **bushbaby**, a small wide-eyed primate named for its cries and cute-looking face. **Hamidi**, a boy from East Africa, enjoys watching the bushbabies leaping great lengths to avoid predators. Later when the blossoms yield gourd-like treats that he calls "monkey bread," Hamidi likes to watch monkeys and baboons bicker as they chomp open the shells to reach the sweet, seed-filled fruit.

The **yagruma** grows along the coasts of the island of Puerto Rico. Its lightweight wood, similar to that of many balsa trees, is used to make baskets, boxes, crates, kites and model airplanes. The **coqui** (KOH-kee) is a tiny tree frog whose name resembles the sound it makes. Coquis are found only in the yagruma forests of Puerto Rico and nowhere else. **Francisca** delights in the sound of the coquis' high-pitched song at night. By day, she enjoys flying simple model airplanes that her Uncle Juan brings from his factory.

A mature **kapok** tree, or silk-cotton tree as it is nicknamed, bears hundreds of six-inch long pods that are filled with fibrous floss. This fiber is buoyant, quick-drying, and moisture-resistant. It is used to stuff pillows, mattresses, life preservers, and cushions, like the kind **Ernesto** from Panama uses. Kapok pods attract many seed-eating animals, including **parakeets**. With their thick beaks, parakeets break open the pods and feast on the seeds attached to the floss.

The **sweetgum** tree is a favorite tree of the **luna**, a large, pale green moth with long-tailed wings marked with purple. The female luna lays eggs in the sweetgum tree so that the larvae can feed upon the leaves when they hatch. The plump green caterpillars with red and purple spots later spin their cocoons on the ground. The sweetgum tree is also a favorite of **John, Amanda, Melissa, Mark** and **Katie** from North Carolina, for the shade and brilliant fall color that it affords.

Virginia Kroll does not do her writing in a secluded cabin or an ivory tower, but in her own home that bustles with the activities of her six children and other members of the household—including many pets. She lives life intensely, and strongly feels a sense of kinship with all life. She is also a prolific writer, at least in the very early hours of the morning when everyone else is asleep. The strength of her compassion and perception come through also in her other books published by Dawn: *Motherlove, With Love to Earth's Endangered Peoples*, and *Cat!*

As a child in school, **Roberta Collier-Morales** peered out the window at the trees and mountains, and filled the margins of her papers—even her tests— with pictures. When her teachers moved her away from the window, she learned to draw from her imagination. She graduated with a degree in illustration from Colorado State University, then taught art in both Colorado and New York City. Now a professional illustrator, she lives with her two children and an extended family in Colorado. She also illustrated *With Love to Earth's Endangered Peoples* for Dawn Publications.

Other books by Virginia Kroll

With Love, to Earth's Endangered Peoples. All over the world, groups of people are in danger of losing their age-old ways forever. Often they have a beautiful, meaningful relationship with Earth. This book portrays several of these peoples, with love.

Motherlove. The love of a mother for her young, it is said, is the closest echo of love divine. This book is a celebration of motherlove—in both animals and humans.

Cat! We humans have a love affair with them. Why? Surely, they are pretty and cute—but there's something more, something uniquely intriguing about cats. Virginia Kroll captures feline essence in this ode to cats.

Other distinctive nature awareness books from Dawn Publications

My Favorite Tree: Terrific Trees of North America, by Diane Iverson. For tree lovers of the 21st century, this book provides both inspiration and a great deal of information about the major native tree species.

The Tree in the Ancient Forest, by Carol Reed-Jones. The amazing ways in which the plants and animals living around a single old fir tree depend upon one another is portrayed in cumulative verse.

Because Brian Hugged His Mother, by David Rice. Brian's hug set in motion a series of unselfish acts that reached more people—and even animals—than he could ever know.

Stickeen: John Muir and the Brave Little Dog, by John Muir as retold by Donnell Rubay. In this classic true story, the relationship between the great naturalist and a small dog is changed forever by their adventure on a glacier in Alaska. Winner of the 1999 Benjamin Franklin Award for nature books.

Dawn Publications is dedicated to inspiring in children a deeper understanding and appreciation for all life on Earth. To order, or for a copy of our catalog, please call 800-545-7475. Please also visit our web site at www.DawnPub.com.